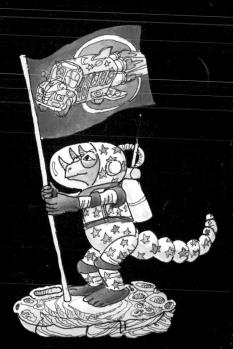

The Magic School Bus
Lost in the Solar System

By Joanna Cole / Illustrated by Bruce Degen

Scholastic Press / New York

The author and illustrator wish to thank Dr. Donna L. Gresh,
Center for Radar Astronomy at Stanford University,
for her assistance in preparing this book.

The author also thanks John Stoke, Astronomical Writer/Producer
at the American Museum-Hayden Planetarium, for his helpful advice,
and Dr. Ellis D. Miner, Cassini Science Manager, Jet Propulsion Laboratory,
for keeping us up-to-date with the latest astronomical measurements.

Library of Congress Cataloging-in-Publication Data
Cole, Joanna
The magic school bus lost in the solar system /
by Joanna Cole; illustrated by Bruce Degen
p. cm
Summary: On a special field trip in the Magic School Bus, Ms. Frizzle's
class goes into outer space and visits each planet in the solar system.
ISBN 0-590-41428-3
1. Outer Space—Exploration— Juvenile literature. 2. Astronomy—
Juvenile literature. [1. Planets. 2. Solar System. 3. Astronomy.]
I. Degen, Bruce, ill. II. Title.
QB500.22.064   1990   523.3   89-10185
CIP   AC

3 4 5 6 7 8 9 10   02 01 0/0

Printed in Mexico   4 9
First edition, October 1990
Revised and updated edition, 1997

The text type was set in 15 point Bookman light.
The illustrator used pen and ink, watercolor, color pencil,
and gouache for the paintings in this book.

To Virginia and Bob McBride—J.C.

For Chris, queen of the
Biscadorian Mother ship—B.D.

Arnold's cousin Janet was
visiting our class for the day.
"I know all of you
will be nice to our guest," said the Friz.

5

We tried to be nice to Janet.
We really did.
As we got on the school bus,
we told her that Ms. Frizzle
is the weirdest teacher in school.
But Janet wasn't interested.
She wanted to tell us about herself.

As usual, it took a while to get the old bus started.
But finally we were on our way.
As we were driving, Ms. Frizzle told us all about how the Earth spins like a top as it moves in its orbit.
It was just a short drive to the planetarium, but Ms. Frizzle talked fast.

THIS BUS IS A WRECK.

AT LEAST IT STARTED THIS TIME.

WE HAVE NEW SCHOOL BUSES AT OUR SCHOOL.

WHAT MAKES NIGHT AND DAY?
by Phoebe
The spinning of the Earth makes night and day.
When one side of the Earth faces the Sun it is daytime on that side. When that side turns away from the Sun, it is night.

WHEN THE EARTH SPINS WE SAY IT ROTATES. THE EARTH MAKES ONE COMPLETE ROTATION— TURN—EVERY 24 HOURS.

When we got to the planetarium,
it was closed for repairs.
"Class, this means we'll
have to return to school,"
said the Friz.
We were so disappointed!

On the way back,
as we were waiting at a red light,
something amazing happened.
The bus started tilting back,
and we heard the roar of rockets.
"Oh, dear," said Ms. Frizzle.
"We seem to be blasting off!"

WHY ARE SPACESHIPS LAUNCHED WITH ROCKETS?
by Wanda

Spaceships cannot just fly into outer space. They need rockets to break free from the powerful grip of Earth's gravity.

WHAT IS GRAVITY?
by Michael

Gravity is the force that pulls objects toward the center of the Earth.

Other planets have gravity, too. Larger planets usually have more gravity. Smaller planets usually have less gravity.

9

The Friz said our first stop
would be the Moon.
We got off the bus and looked around.
There was no air, no water,
no sign of life.
All we saw were dust and rock
and lots and lots of craters.
Ms. Frizzle said the craters were
formed billions of years ago
when the Moon was hit by meteorites.
Meteorites are falling chunks
of rock and metal.

WE ARE SO LIGHT ON THE MOON!

THAT'S BECAUSE THE MOON HAS LESS GRAVITY THAN THE EARTH.

YOUR WEIGHT AND FATE ON THE MOON

lbs. 85 Earth Weight	lbs. 14 Moon Weight

You will travel to far off places.

It was fun on the Moon.
We wanted to play,
but Ms. Frizzle said it was time to go.
So we got back on the bus.
"We'll start with the Sun,
the center of the solar system,"
said the Friz, and we blasted off.

LOOK HOW HIGH WE CAN JUMP!

I WAS IN A NATIONAL JUMP-ROPE CONTEST. I WON, OF COURSE.

IS THERE A NATIONAL BRAGGING CONTEST?

WHAT MAKES THE MOON SHINE?
by Rachel
The Moon does not make any light of its own. The moonlight we see from Earth is really light from the sun. It hits the Moon and bounces off, the way light is reflected from a mirror.

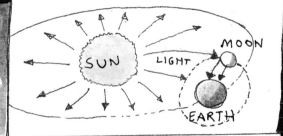

THE MOON'S ORBIT
by Amanda Jane
The Moon travels in orbit around the Earth, just as the Earth travels around the Sun.

13

THE SUN IS A STAR
by Carmen
Our Sun is an average star like the ones we see in the night sky.

WHICH STAR DO WE SEE ONLY IN THE DAYTIME?

THAT'S EASY: THE SUN.

HOW BIG IS THE SUN?
by Gregory
Our sun measures more than a million kilometers across. More than one million Earths could fit inside it!

We zoomed toward the Sun, the biggest, brightest, and hottest object in the solar system.
Jets of super-hot gases shot out at us from the surface.
Thank goodness Ms. Frizzle didn't get *too* close!

YOU SHOULD NEVER LOOK DIRECTLY AT THE SUN, CHILDREN. IT CAN DAMAGE YOUR EYES!

YOU SHOULD NEVER DRIVE A BUS DIRECTLY INTO THE SUN, EITHER!

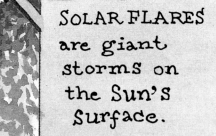

SOLAR FLARES are giant storms on the Sun's surface.

She steered around to the other side and pulled away.

"We'll be seeing all the planets in order, class," explained Frizzie. "Mercury is the first planet, the closest to the Sun."

MY SCHOOL IS HEATED WITH SOLAR ENERGY.

I HAVE A SUN DECK.

I HAVE TEN PAIRS OF SUNGLASSES.

GIVE US A BREAK, JANET.

HOW HOT IS THE SUN?
by Florrie
At the center of the sun the temperature is about 15 million degrees Celsius!

The sun is so hot it heats planets that are millions of kilometers away.

SUN SPOTS are areas that are cooler than the rest of the Sun.

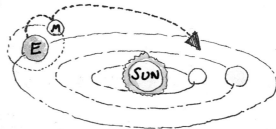
Our Path So Far

Mercury was a dead, sun-baked planet.
"This planet is a lot like our Moon.
There is no water and hardly any air,"
said the Friz.
"Notice the craters on its surface
as we pass by."

THE SUN LOOKS TWICE AS BIG HERE AS IT DOES FROM EARTH.

THAT'S BECAUSE MERCURY IS SO CLOSE.

TOO CLOSE! LET'S GO!

YOUR WEIGHT AND FATE ON MERCURY

| lbs. 85 Earth Weight | lbs. 32 Mercury Weight |

You will Vacation in a Sunny Spot.

Before long, we felt ourselves being pulled in by the gravity of Venus —the second planet from the Sun. Venus was completely covered by a thick layer of yellowish clouds. "We will now explore the surface of Venus," said Ms. Frizzle.

WHY IS IT SO HOT ON VENUS?
by Ralph
Venus's atmosphere has a lot of carbon dioxide gas in it. Carbon dioxide acts like a blanket to hold heat in.

CLOUDS
HEAT
HEAT
HEAT

When heat is trapped like this by a planet's atmosphere, it is called the "greenhouse effect."

Below the clouds, Venus was as dry as a desert.
The ground was covered with rocks.
And it was HOT!
It was about 460 degrees Celsius!
That's *much* hotter than an oven baking cookies!

THERE'S NO LIFE ON VENUS, CLASS.

IT'S TOO HOT!

IT'S TOO DRY!

THERE'S TOO MUCH ACID!

LET'S LEAVE!

18

The air was so heavy
we could feel it pressing down on us!
Ms. Frizzle said there are active volcanoes
around, too.
We said, "Let's get out of here!"
"Our next stop is Mars,
the red planet, fourth from the Sun,"
announced the Friz.
"On our way, we'll be passing through
the orbit of Earth, the third planet."
The bus lifted off with a roar.

IT NEVER RAINS
ON VENUS
by Dorothy Ann
Venus's clouds
never make rain
because it is too hot
for rain to form. Any
liquid on Venus dries
up instantly.

I'VE BEEN TO MARS
LOTS OF TIMES.

JUST
IGNORE HER.

Our Path So Far

WHY AREN'T MARS'S
MOONS ROUND?
by John
Large moons are
round because of
their gravity. Billions
of years ago, when
large moons formed,
their gravity pulled
in their material evenly
and made them round.
    The moons of Mars
are so small that

they don't have
enough gravity
to be round.

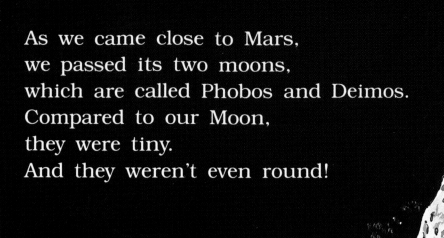

As we came close to Mars,
we passed its two moons,
which are called Phobos and Deimos.
Compared to our Moon,
they were tiny.
And they weren't even round!

Phobos
(18 miles long)

Deimos
(9 miles long)

Volcano

LONG AGO, THERE
MAY HAVE BEEN
WATER IN THOSE
CHANNELS,

YES, BUT TODAY
ALL MARS'S WATER
IS FROZEN IN
THE POLAR
ICE CAPS.

THOSE ARE
MOONS?

THEY LOOK LIKE
POTATOES
WITH CRATERS.

20

Looking down, we saw a huge canyon.
Ms. Frizzle said it was
as long as the United States.
There was a volcano
three times taller than
the tallest volcano on Earth.
And all around, there were channels
that looked like dried-up river beds.

Is THERE LIFE ON MARS?
by Molly
No life has been
found on Mars.
Living things need
water, and there
is no liquid water
on Mars.
So space scientists
think life probably
cannot exist there!

Polar Ice Cap

Canyon

Channels

YOUR WEIGHT AND FATE ON MARS

lbs.	lbs.
85	32
Earth Weight	Mars Weight

EARTH IS THE
BEST PLANET FOR
LIFE. THAT'S WHY
I LIVE THERE.

Things will
look rosy
soon.

JANET LIKES TO
BE THE BEST.

WE NOTICED.

"Mars is the last of what we call
the inner planets!"
Ms. Frizzle shouted above the roar of the rockets.
"We will now be going
through the asteroid belt
to the outer planets!"

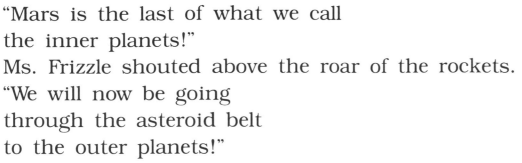

ISN'T SPACE TRAVEL EXCITING, ARNOLD?

I REALLY PREFER FILMSTRIPS.

AIR LOCK
KEEP THIS DOOR CLOSED

EXIT

Our Path So Far

Asteroid Belt

THE ASTEROID BELT
by Shirley

The area between the inner and the outer planets is called the asteroid belt. It is filled with thousands and thousands of asteroids.

WHAT ARE ASTEROIDS?
by Florrie

Asteroids are chunks of rock and metal in orbit around the sun. They may be building blocks of a planet that never formed. Or they could be pieces of planets that broke apart.

Thousands of asteroids were spinning all around us.
All at once, we heard the tinkling of broken glass.
One of our taillights had been hit by an asteroid.
Ms. Frizzle put the bus on autopilot and went out to take a look.
She kept on talking about asteroids over the bus radio.

THE LARGEST ASTEROID IS ONLY $\frac{1}{3}$ THE SIZE OF OUR MOON. MOST ASTEROIDS ARE THE SIZE OF HOUSES OR SMALLER.

I WISH SHE'D COME INSIDE.

Suddenly there was a snap.
Ms. Frizzle's tether line had broken!
Without warning,
the rockets fired up,
and the bus zoomed away!
The autopilot was malfunctioning.

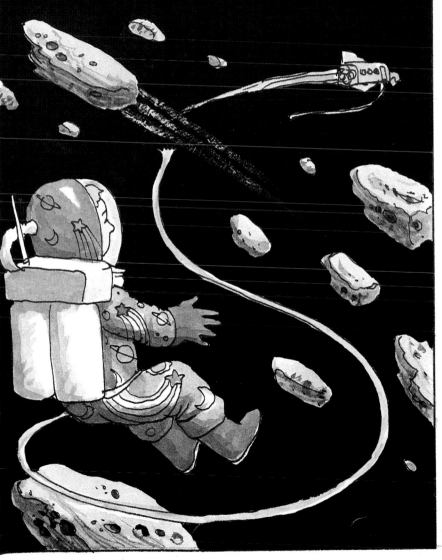

On the radio, Ms. Frizzle's voice grew
fainter and fainter.
Then she was gone.
We were on our own!
We were lost in the solar system!

25

Most of us were too scared to move.
But Janet started searching the bus.
In the glove compartment
she found Ms. Frizzle's lesson book.
As she began reading from it,
a huge planet came into view.
"Class, this is Jupiter," Janet read.
"It's the first of the outer planets,
and the largest planet in the solar system."

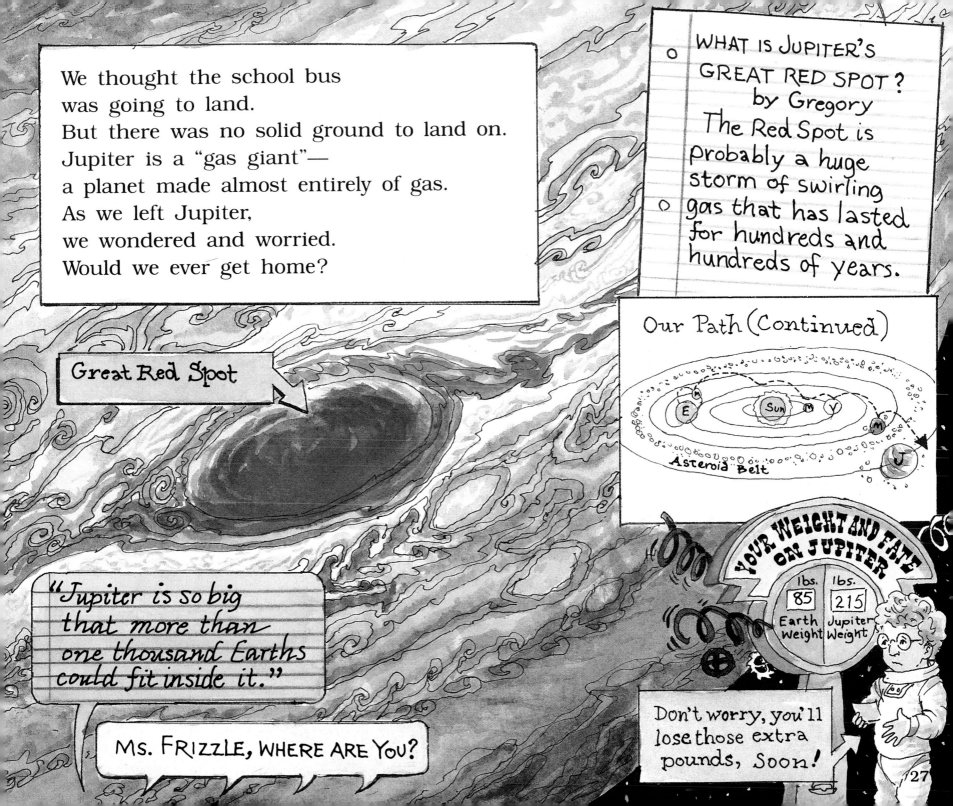

We thought the school bus
was going to land.
But there was no solid ground to land on.
Jupiter is a "gas giant"—
a planet made almost entirely of gas.
As we left Jupiter,
we wondered and worried.
Would we ever get home?

WHAT IS JUPITER'S
GREAT RED SPOT?
by Gregory

The Red Spot is probably a huge storm of swirling gas that has lasted for hundreds and hundreds of years.

Great Red Spot

Our Path (Continued)

Sun

Asteroid Belt

"Jupiter is so big that more than one thousand Earths could fit inside it."

MS. FRIZZLE, WHERE ARE YOU?

YOUR WEIGHT AND FATE ON JUPITER

lbs. 85
Earth Weight

lbs. 215
Jupiter Weight

Don't worry, you'll lose those extra pounds, soon!

The next sight made us forget our troubles.
It was Saturn, a gas planet like Jupiter.
It had swirling clouds and lots of moons.
But the most incredible thing about Saturn
was its rings.
It was the most beautiful planet
in the solar system!

29

THE TIPPED OVER PLANET
by Ralph
Uranus spins differently from the other planets.
It seems to be lying on its side compared to most other planets in the Solar System.

Uranus Earth Sun

YOUR WEIGHT AND FATE ON URANUS

lbs. 85	lbs. 77
Earth Weight	Uranus Weight

Feeling blue? You may be homesick.

Next was Uranus, a blue-green gas planet with faint gray rings and moons.
Some scientists think they might be made of chunks of graphite—
the material used in pencils on Earth.

"Methane gas in its atmosphere makes Uranus look blue."

YOU LOOK KIND OF BLUE YOURSELF.

I'M FREEZING!

THAT'S BECAUSE WE'RE SO FAR AWAY FROM THE SUN.

The bus was going faster and faster,
and we couldn't control the autopilot.
We swept past stormy Neptune,
another blue-green planet—eighth from the Sun.
All we could think about
was finding Ms. Frizzle!

"Neptune is the last of the giant gas planets."

WE'RE ALMOST OUT OF GAS OURSELVES!

Great Dark Spot

AND THE NEAREST SERVICE STATION IS 4,000 MILLION KILOMETERS AWAY.

YOUR WEIGHT AND FATE ON NEPTUNE

| lbs. 85 Earth Weight | lbs. 97 Neptune Weight |

You will have a happy birthday 165 years from now.

IS PLUTO A REAL PLANET?
by Wanda
Some scientists think Pluto was once a moon of Neptune. It may have escaped from the orbit around Neptune. Then it became a real planet in orbit around the Sun. Pluto was the last planet discovered in the known Solar system.

YOUR WEIGHT AND FATE ON PLUTO

lbs.	lbs.
85	6
Earth Weight	Pluto Weight

You will meet a small, dark planet.

We were going so fast,
we almost missed seeing the ninth planet,
tiny Pluto,* and its moon, Charon.
We were so far away from the Sun that it
didn't look big anymore.
It just looked like a very bright star.
We were leaving the solar system.

*Every 248 years, Neptune's orbit is further out than Pluto's. Then Neptune is the ninth planet. But most of the time, Pluto is the ninth planet from the Sun.

THERE'S NOTHING OUT THERE — BUT STARS.

MAYBE THERE'S A TENTH PLANET WAITING TO BE DISCOVERED.

IT'LL HAVE TO WAIT.

I HOPE MS. FRIZZLE IS WAITING, TOO.

CHARON

PLUTO

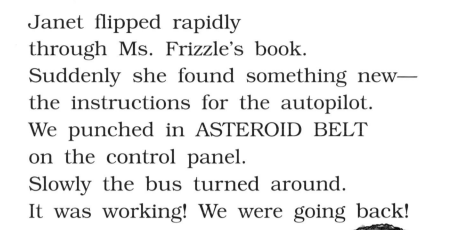

Janet flipped rapidly
through Ms. Frizzle's book.
Suddenly she found something new—
the instructions for the autopilot.
We punched in ASTEROID BELT
on the control panel.
Slowly the bus turned around.
It was working! We were going back!

JANET REALLY SAVED THE DAY.

I TOLD YOU SHE'S A GOOD KID.

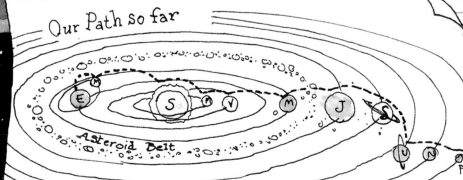

Our Path so far

Asteroid Belt

33

With Frizzie back at the wheel,
the bus headed straight for Earth.
We reentered the atmosphere,
landed with a thump,
and looked around.

We were in the school parking lot again.
The rockets were gone.
The space suits were gone.
The bus was a wreck.
Everything was back to normal.

35

OUR PLANET CHART

PLANET	HOW BIG ACROSS	HOW LONG ONE ROTATION	HOW LONG ONE YEAR	HOW FAR FROM THE SUN (AVERAGE)	HOW MANY KNOWN MOONS	ARE THERE RINGS?
MERCURY	4,878 km.	58.6 days	88.0 Earth days	57.9 million Km.	None	No
VENUS	12,104 km.	243.0 days	224.7 Earth days	108.2 million Km.	None	No
EARTH	12,756 km.	23.9 hours	365.3 Earth days	149.6 million Km.	1	No
MARS	6,794 km.	24.6 hours	687.0 Earth days	227.9 million km.	2	No
JUPITER	142,984 km.	9.9 hours	11.9 Earth years	778.3 million km.	16	Yes
SATURN	120,536 km.	10.7 hours	29.5 Earth years	1,429.4 million km.	18	Yes
URANUS	51,118 km.	17.2 hours	84.0 Earth years	2,871.0 million km.	15	Yes
NEPTUNE	49,528 km.	16.1 hours	164.8 Earth Years	4,504.3 million km.	8	Yes
PLUTO	about 2,300 km.	6.4 days	248.6 Earth years	5,913.5 million km.	1	No

In the classroom,
we made a terrific
chart of the planets
and a mobile of the solar system.

At last, it was time to go home.
It had been a typical day
in Ms. Frizzle's class.
Now we had only one problem.
Would anyone ever believe us
when we told about our trip?

ATTENTION, READERS!

<u>DO NOT</u> ATTEMPT THIS TRIP ON YOUR OWN SCHOOL BUS!

Three reasons why not:

1. Attaching rockets to your school bus will upset your teacher, the school principal, and your parents. It will not get you into orbit anyway. An ordinary bus cannot travel in outer space, and you cannot become astronauts without years of training.

2. Landing on certain planets may be dangerous to your health. Even astronauts cannot visit Venus (it's too hot), Mercury (it's too close to the Sun), or Jupiter (its gravity would crush human beings). People cannot fly to the Sun, either. Its gravity and heat would be too strong.

3. Space travel could make you miss dinner with your family... for the rest of your childhood. Even if a school bus <u>could</u> go to outer space, it could never travel through the entire solar system in one day. It took <u>years</u> for the Voyager space probes to do that.

ON THE OTHER HAND...

If a red-haired teacher in a funny dress shows up at your school — start packing!